PRESENTS

learn
Rock Guitar

BEGINNER

Method by John McCarthy

Written and Adapted by Steve Gorenberg

Supervising Editor: Joe Palombo
Production Manager: Tara Altamuro
Layout, Graphics and Design: Steve Gorenberg
Photography: Nick Finelli
Audio Engineer: Jimmy Rutkowski

Copy Editors and Proofreaders:
Alex Palombo, Irene Villaverde

Cover Art Direction and Design:
Paul Enea, Tovero & Marks

ISBN: 978-0-9789832-3-9

Produced by The Rock House Method®

Table of Contents

About the Author

John McCarthy
Creator of
the Rock House Method

John is the creator of **The Rock House Method**®, the world's leading musical instruction system. Over his 20 year career, he has produced and/or appeared in more than 100 instructional products. Millions of people around the world have learned to play music using John's easy to follow, accelerated program.

John is a virtuoso guitarist who has worked with some of the industry's most legendary musicians. He has the ability to break down, teach and communicate music in a manner that motivates and inspires others to achieve their dreams of playing an instrument.

As a guitarist and songwriter, John blends together a unique style of Rock, Metal, Funk and Blues in a collage of melodic compositions, jam-packed with masterful guitar techniques. His sound has been described as a combination of vintage guitar rock with a progressive, gritty edge that is perfectly suited for today's audiences.

Throughout his career, John has recorded and performed with renowned musicians like Doug Wimbish (who has worked with Joe Satriani, Living Colour, The Rolling Stones, Madonna, Annie Lennox and many more top flight artists), Grammy winner Leo Nocentelli, Rock & Roll Hall of Fame inductees Bernie Worrell and Jerome "Big Foot" Brailey, Freekbass, Gary Hoey, Bobby Kimball, David Ellefson (founding member of seven time Grammy nominee Megadeth), Will Calhoun (who has worked with B.B. King, Mick Jagger and Paul Simon), Jordan Giangreco from the acclaimed band The Breakfast, and solo artist Alex Bach. John has also shared the stage with Blue Oyster Cult, Randy Bachman, Marc Rizzo, Jerry Donahue, Bernard Fowler, Stevie Salas, Brian Tichy, Kansas, Al Dimeola and Dee Snyder.

For more information on John, his music and his instructional products visit www.rockhousemethod.com.

CREATING MUSICIANS
ONE LESSON AT A TIME

Introduction

Welcome to **The Rock House Method**® system of learning. You are joining millions of aspiring musicians around the world who use our easy-to-understand methods for learning to play music.

Unlike conventional learning programs, **The Rock House Method**® is a four-part teaching system that employs DVD, CD and 24/7 online lesson support along with this book to give you a variety of sources to assure a complete learning experience. The products can be used individually or together. The DVD that comes with this book matches the curriculum exactly, providing you with a live instructor for visual reference. In addition, the DVD contains some valuable extras like sections on changing your strings, guitar care and an interactive chord library. The CD that we've included lets you take your lessons with you anywhere you go.

How to Use the Lesson Support Site

Every Rock House product offers FREE membership to our interactive Lesson Support site. Use the member number included with your book to register at www.rockhousemethod.com. You will find your member number on the sleeve that contains your DVD and CD. Once registered, you can use this fully interactive site along with your product to enhance your learning experience, expand your knowledge, link with instructors, and connect with a community of people around the world who are learning to play music using **The Rock House Method**®. There are sections that directly correspond to this product within the *Additional Information* and *Backing Tracks* sections. There are also a variety of other tools you can utilize such as *Ask The Teacher*, *Quizzes*, *Reference Material*, *Definitions*, *Forums*, *Live Chats*, *Guitar Professor* and much more.

ICON KEY

Throughout this book, you'll periodically notice the following icons. They indicate when there are additional learning tools available on our support website for the section you're working on. When you see an icon in the book, visit the member section of www.rockhousemethod.com for musical backing tracks, additional information and learning utilities.

CD Track Number

The accompanying CD includes lesson demonstrations, additional information and bass and drum backing tracks. When you see a CD icon and track number, follow along with the included CD to hear the examples and play along. A complete track listing is also included in the back of this book.

Backing Track

Many of the exercises in this book are intended to be played along with bass and drum rhythm tracks. This icon indicates that there is a backing track available for download on the Lesson Support Site.

Additional Information

The question mark icon indicates there is more information for that section available on the website. It can be theory, more playing examples, or tips.

Metronome

Metronome icons are placed next to the examples that we recommend you practice using a metronome. You can download a free, adjustable metronome from the support site.

Tablature

This icon indicates that there is additional guitar tablature available on the website that corresponds to the lesson. There is also an extensive database of tab music online that is updated regularly.

Tuner

Also found on the website is free tuner software which you can download to help you tune your instrument.

The **D** and **E** chords are easier to play than the previous chords. They are also two of the most commonly used open major chords. Neither chord uses the fourth finger and all of the fretted notes are on adjacent strings, making it easier to play them cleanly.

D

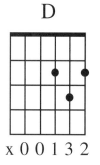

x 0 0 1 3 2

E

023100

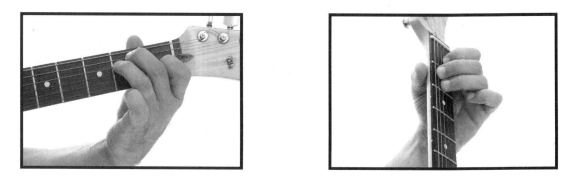

The last two open major chords in this section are the **F** and **G** chords. The **F** chord is especially difficult to play because you need to barre the highest two strings with your first finger and put your second and third fingers down straight. If you tilt your first finger barre to the left side, it makes it easier to fret the other notes properly. Pick each note out individually to make sure the chord sounds clean and that you're playing it correctly. Once you've memorized all of the open major chords, practice changing from chord to chord efficiently.

F

x x 3 2 1 1

G

210034

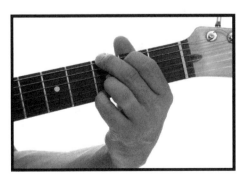

Lesson 6

Picking Exercise

Here's an alternate picking exercise to help coordinate your right hand. Instead of strumming the chords, you might pick the notes of a chord out individually and let them ring out together. The following symbols indicate whether a note is picked in an up or a down direction:

⊓ - downpick (pick down toward the floor)

∨ - uppick (pick up toward the ceiling)

Fret an open D chord and hold the chord shape with your left hand while picking out the individual notes in the order indicated below. This picking pattern (indicated by which number string you pick) is 4 - 1 - 3 - 1 - 2 - 1. Recite the string number while you pick each one to help memorize the order. Use a down-up-down-up alternate picking pattern. Notice that the 1st string is always uppicked, while the other strings are all downpicked. Try to hold one of your right hand fingers on the body of the guitar to help give you added support and control. Practice playing in a steady, even rhythm, in time with a metronome.

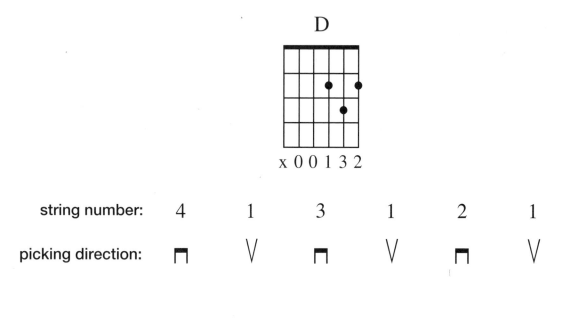

Quick Tip!

choose your teacher wisely

Finding a good guitar teacher is essential, especially for beginners. Playing well and teaching well are separate skills. Just because someone can play guitar doesn't automatically mean they have the proper skills to teach guitar. Before you commit to a teacher, you may want to ask for a trial lesson to make sure you're happy with the communication skills and the teaching method the instructor provides. If you're not learning from someone who knows how to teach, you may have a difficult time.

Lesson 7

Basic Strumming

Once you have the chords sounding clean and the strumming motion down, the next step is to learn how to change chords quickly and cleanly. Focus on where each finger needs to move for the next chord. Sometimes one or more of your fingers will be able to stay in the same place. Avoid taking your hand completely off the neck. Instead, try to move your whole hand as little as possible and make smaller finger adjustments to change from one chord to the next. When you can change from chord to chord seamlessly, you'll be able to play complete songs.

Strumming Pattern #1

The following is an example of a *chord progression* and is written on a musical *staff*. A staff is the group of horizontal lines on which music is written. The chord names above the staff show which chord to play, and the *rhythm slashes* indicate the rhythm in which the chords are strummed. A chord progression is a series of chords played in a specified rhythm and order. In this chord progression, strum each chord four times, using all downstrums. This example also uses *repeat signs* (play through the progression and repeat it again). Keep practicing and try to change chords in time without stalling or missing a beat. Count along out loud with each strum, in time and on the beat. Start out slowly if you need to and gradually get it up to speed.

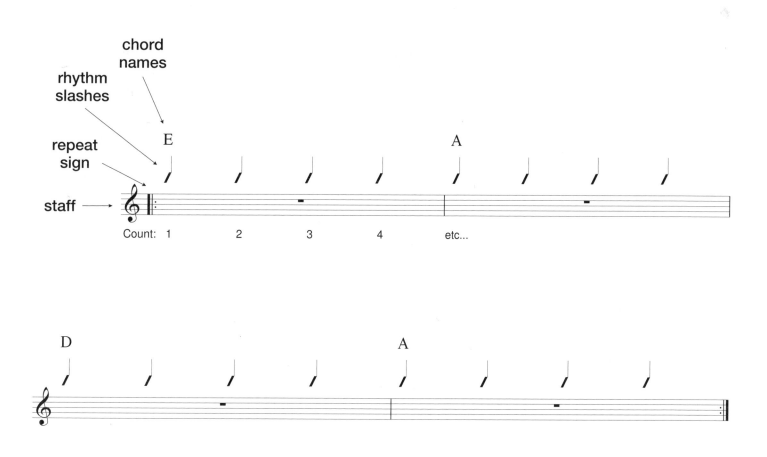

19

Rhythm Notation

You don't need to read traditional music notation in order to play guitar, but it's helpful to understand a little bit about the concept of rhythm and timing. In most popular rock and blues, music is divided into *measures* of four beats. When a band counts off "One, two, three, four" at the beginning of a song, it represents one complete measure of music. Different types of notes are held for different durations within a measure. For example, a *quarter note* gets one beat because a quarter note is held for one quarter of a measure.

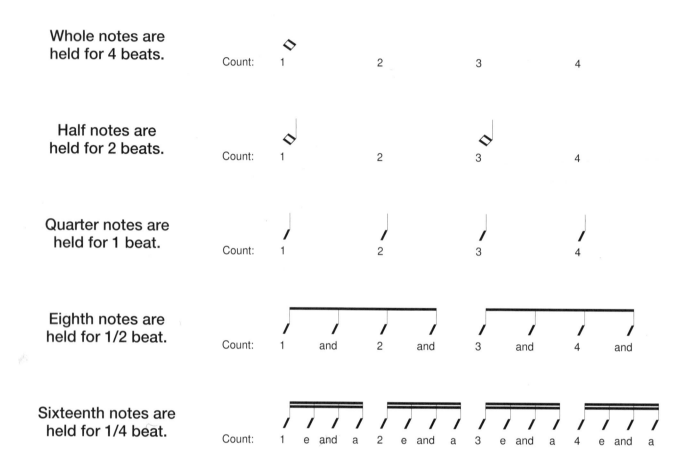

A *tie* is a curved line connecting one note to the next. If two notes are tied, strike only the first one and let it ring out through the duration of the second note (or "tied" note).

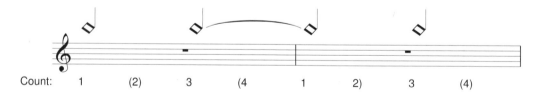

A *dot* after a note increases its value by another 1/2 of its original value. In the following example the half notes are dotted, so they are held for three beats.

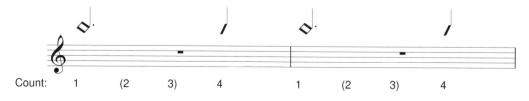

Strumming Pattern #2

The following strumming pattern uses another new chord, the **Cadd9** chord. A Cadd9 chord (or a Csus2 chord) is a slight variation of the regular C chord. Notice how similar the fingering is to the G chord and how easy it is to switch back and forth between them. Just leave your third and fourth fingers stationary and move your first and second fingers up or down one string.

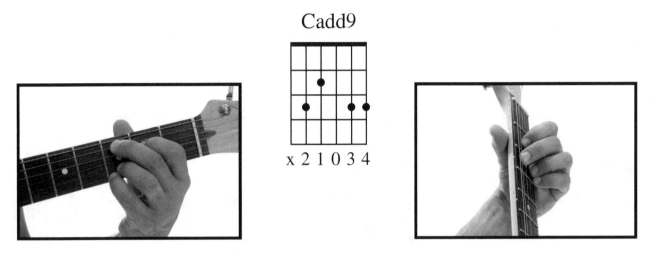

Cadd9

x 2 1 0 3 4

This exercise utilizes a strumming technique that we call a *ghost strum*. A ghost strum occurs when you move the pick over the strings without actually striking them. This allows you to keep your arm moving in a constant down-up-down motion, keeping your playing fluid and in time. The strumming symbols in parentheses indicate where ghost strums occur.

The rhythm used is an example of *syncopation*. You're playing a syncopated rhythm if there's one or more strums off the beat, or on the upbeat instead of the downbeat. The strum on beat 2 1/2 is tied to beat 3, so you don't strum directly on beat 3.

If you're having trouble changing from chord to chord smoothly, isolate the change and just practice going back and forth between those two chords. With practice, you'll build finger memory and your fingers will instinctively know where to go. Play this rhythm along with the backing track and get the changes, the feel and the strumming motion down.

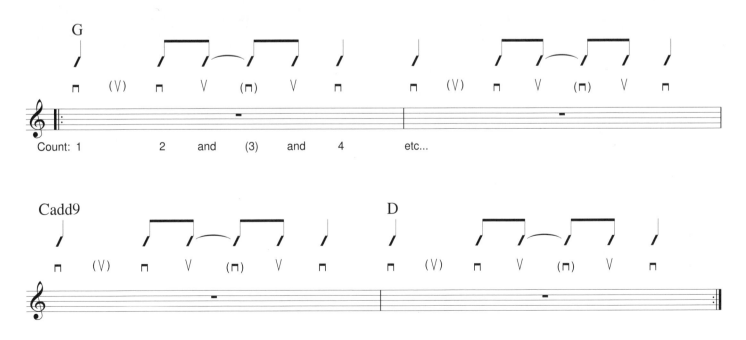

Review Quiz #1

1) The fretboard is a component of which part of the guitar?
   A. the body
   B. the headstock
   C. the neck
   D. the strap

2) The names of the open strings, from lowest to highest pitched, are:
   A. B-E-G-A-D-E
   B. A-G-E-B-E-D
   C. E-A-D-G-B-E
   D. A-B-C-D-E-F

3) A barre is executed by
   A. placing one finger flat across more than one string
   B. playing all the notes of a chord separately
   C. holding the guitar upside down
   D. holding the pick between your index finger and thumb

4) A series of chords played in a specified rhythm and order is called a
   A. song
   B. chord diagram
   C. chord progression
   D. symphony

5) Quarter notes are held for
   A. one quarter of a beat
   B. four beats
   C. one beat
   D. a quarter of a second

6) Consistent down-up-down-up picking is called
   A. alternative picking
   B. up and down picking
   C. alternate picking
   D. back and forth picking

7) The two major open chords that require you to barre more than one note are
   A. C and G
   B. A and F
   C. D and E
   D. G and B

8) A ghost strum occurs
   A. when you drop the pick
   B. when you're playing minor chords
   C. when your strumming hand passes over the strings in time without striking them
   D. when you play so fast, your hand is invisible like a ghost

Answers to the review quiz are located on page 63.

Lesson 8

Tablature Explanation

Tablature (or *tab*) is a number system for reading notes on the neck of a guitar. It does not require you to have knowledge of standard music notation. This system was designed specifically for the guitar. Most music for guitar is available in tab. Tablature is a crucial and essential part of your guitar playing career.

The six lines of the tablature staff represent each of the six strings. The top line is the thinnest (highest pitched) string. The bottom line is the thickest (lowest pitched) string. The lines in between are the 2nd through 5th strings. The numbers placed directly on these lines show you the fret number to play the note at. At the bottom, underneath the staff, is a series of numbers. These numbers show you which left hand fingers you should use to fret the notes.

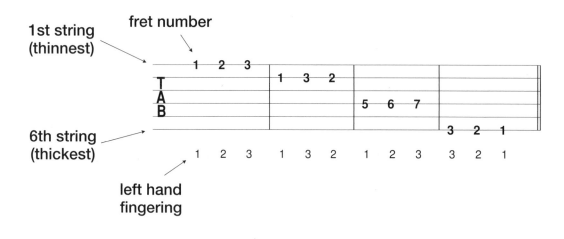

Chords can also be written in tab. If there are several numbers stacked together in a column, those notes should be played or strummed at the same time. Here are the seven major open chords you already know from the previous section with the tablature written out underneath each diagram. Since the fingerings are shown on the chord diagrams, we won't bother to repeat them underneath the tab.

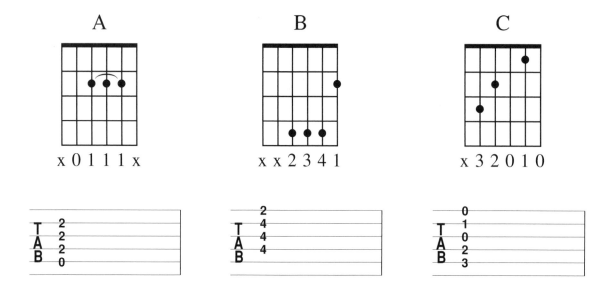

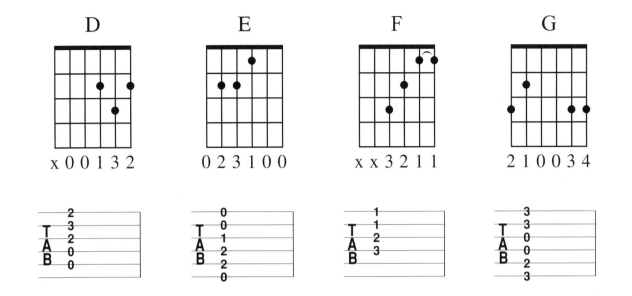

Lesson 9
Finger Exercise #1

This is a finger exercise in tablature that will build coordination and strengthen your fingers. It's designed to help stretch your hand out, so keep your fingers spread across the first four frets, one finger per fret. Leave your first finger anchored in place and reach for the following three notes by stretching your hand out.

With your right hand, use alternate picking in a consistent down-up-down-up pendulum motion. Alternate picking will help develop speed, smoothness and technique. Practice this exercise using the metronome for timing and control.

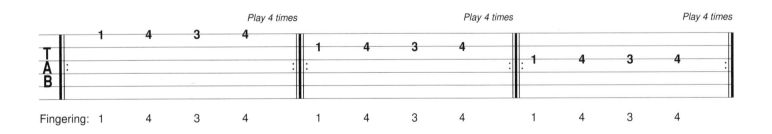

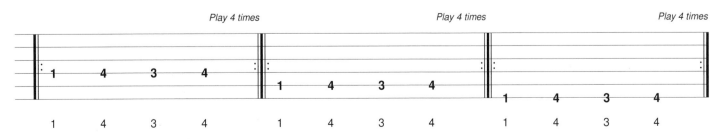

Lesson 10

Blues Rhythm #1

The following is a basic blues riff in the key of A. This riff is made up of two note chords shown on the tab staff. The chord names above the staff are there as a reference to show you what the basic harmony is while you play along.

This riff should sound very familiar - it's used more than any other blues progression. Plenty of rock and blues classics are played entirely with this one riff repeated over and over. It is made up of 12 measures (or *bars*) of music called the *12-bar blues*, a blues progression consisting of twelve repeated bars of music.

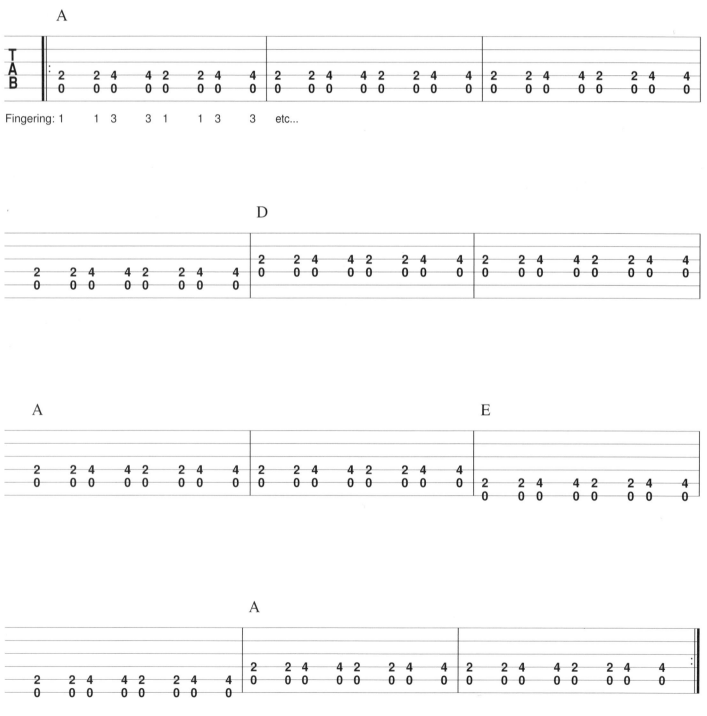

Blues is played with a *shuffle feel*, also called a triplet feel. This example was written in eighth notes and the second eighth note of each beat should lag a little. This is referred to as triplet feel because the beat is actually divided by thirds, counted as if there were three eighth notes per beat instead of two. The first part of the beat gets 2/3 of a beat and the second part only gets 1/3.

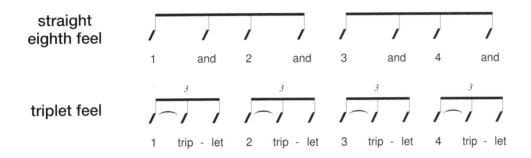

Shuffle feel is a much easier concept to understand by hearing it. Listen to the backing track, count along and try to get the triplet feel in your head. Also, check out almost any blues standard, slow or fast and you'll probably recognize a shuffle feel being used.

This 12-bar blues riff is also an example of a **I - IV - V** (one - four - five) chord progression. The Roman numerals refer to the steps of the scale, relative to what key the music is in. This blues riff is in the key of A, so the A chord is the **I** chord (also called the *tonic*). The D chord is the **IV** chord (also called the *subdominant*) because in the key of A, D is the fourth step of the scale. Finally, the **V** chord (or *dominant*) is the E chord, because E is the fifth step of the scale in the key of A.

The I - IV - V chord progression is the most common progression used in rock or blues. It's the foundation that all rock and blues was built on and has evolved from. There are many variations, but songs such as "Johnny B. Goode," "You Really Got Me," "Rock and Roll," "I Love Rock and Roll" and "Sympathy for the Devil" are all based on the I - IV - V.

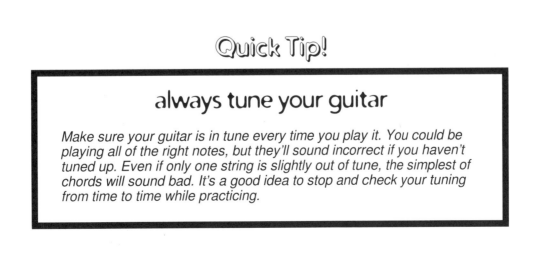

Quick Tip!

always tune your guitar

Make sure your guitar is in tune every time you play it. You could be playing all of the right notes, but they'll sound incorrect if you haven't tuned up. Even if only one string is slightly out of tune, the simplest of chords will sound bad. It's a good idea to stop and check your tuning from time to time while practicing.

Lesson 11

Minor Open Chords

Minor chords have a sad or melancholy sound, whereas major chords have a happy or bright sound.
In this section we'll learn the seven popular minor open (or 1st position) chords. A lowercase "m" within
a chord name indicates a minor chord.

Am

x 0 2 3 1 0

Am

```
    0
T   1
A   2
B   2
    0
```

Bm

x x 3 4 2 1

Bm

```
    2
T   3
A   4
B   4
```

Notice that the **Bm** and **Cm** chords both have the exact same fingering. To go from **Bm** to **Cm**,
simply slide your hand up the neck one fret to the 3rd fret (indicated by the 3fr. just to the left of
the **Cm** chord diagram).

Cm

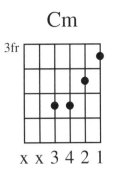

3fr

x x 3 4 2 1

Cm

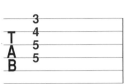

```
    3
  T 4
  A 5
  B 5
```

Dm

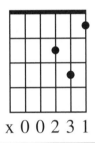

x 0 0 2 3 1

Dm

```
    1
  T 3
  A 2
  B 0
    0
```

Em

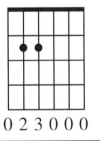

0 2 3 0 0 0

Em

```
    0
  T 0
  A 0
  B 2
    2
    0
```

Here's an alternate fingering for the **Em** chord using the first and second fingers. Depending on the context in which it's used in a chord progression, it might be easier to change from chord to chord by slightly varying the fingering. Both fingerings of the chord are useful to know.

Em

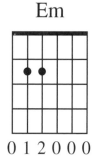

0 1 2 0 0 0

The **Fm** and **Gm** chords contain a first finger barre and also use identical fingerings; **Fm** is played at the 1st fret, and **Gm** is played one whole step higher at the 3rd fret.

Fm

x x 3 1 1 1

Fm

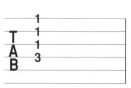

Gm

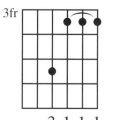
3fr

x x 3 1 1 1

Gm

Lesson 12
Open Chord Rhythm

This chord progression combines both major and minor chords in the key of A minor. The four chords used in the progression are shown in order using chord diagrams below. Use the alternate fingering for the Em chord (with your first and second fingers) to make changing from chord to chord easier. Notice how similar the fingerings are between the Am and C chords; simply move your third finger and leave your other fingers stationary. Play along with the backing track and practice changing chords cleanly and in time. Use the strumming pattern indicated by the symbols above the tab staff.

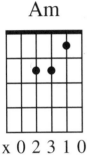
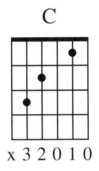
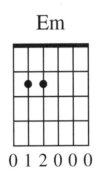
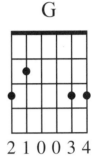

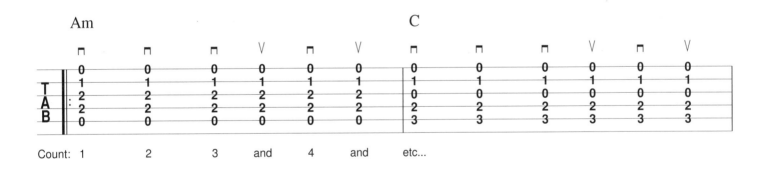

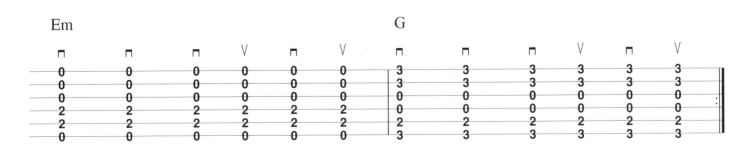

Lesson 13
Finger Exercise #2

This is a finger exercise in tablature that will build coordination and strengthen your left hand. Fret each note individually, using one finger at a time. Play each measure four times, then proceed to the next measure without pausing. This will help build endurance. Use alternate picking and practice this exercise using the metronome for timing and control.

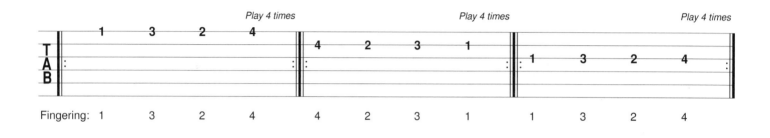

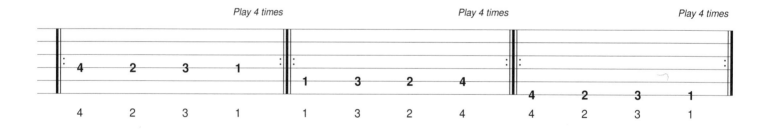

Quick Tip!

make sure your guitar is set up properly

Beginners don't usually realize that their new guitars may need to be set up to play comfortably. A proper set up will ensure that the strings are at the correct height. If they're too high off the neck, it will be harder to press the strings down. You'll also want to check the neck adjustment to be sure your guitar neck has the proper curve. Even right out of the box, new guitars need adjusting. This oversight can cause many beginners to give up in frustration before giving it a fair chance on a properly adjusted instrument.

Lesson 14
Minor Pentatonic Scales 1 – 3

Minor pentatonic scales are the most commonly used scales for playing rock and blues solos.
The pentatonic is a five note scale, or an abbreviated version of the full natural minor scale.
The word "pentatonic" comes from the greek words, "penta" (five) and "tonic" (the keynote).

Here is the A minor pentatonic scale shown in tab. Practice the scale ascending and descending
using consistent alternate picking. Memorize this scale; it's the one you'll use most often for playing
melodies and leads.

1st Position A Minor Pentatonic Scale (Ascending)

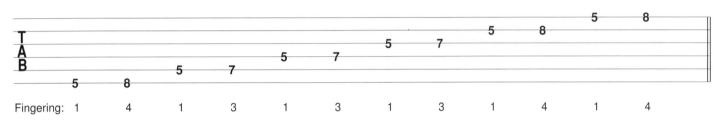

Fingering: 1   4   1   3   1   3   1   3   1   4   1   4

1st Position A Minor Pentatonic Scale (Descending)

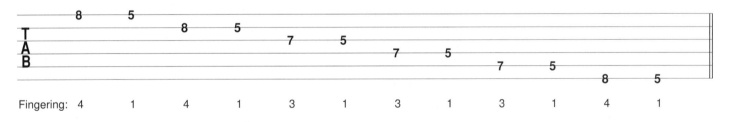

Fingering: 4   1   4   1   3   1   3   1   3   1   4   1

Scale Diagrams

Here is a scale diagram which is similar to the chord diagrams you've already seen. A scale diagram shows
all the notes in the scale within a certain position on the neck. This diagram is for the 1st position A minor
pentatonic scale you've just learned. The stacked numbers below indicate the fingering for the notes
on each string.

**1st position
A minor pentatonic scale**

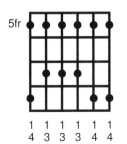

Here are two more positions of the A minor pentatonic scale. Knowing the different positions of the minor pentatonic scale allows you to play leads anywhere on the neck. There are a total of five positions, each position starting on a different note of the scale.

2nd Position A Minor Pentatonic Scale (Ascending)

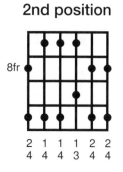

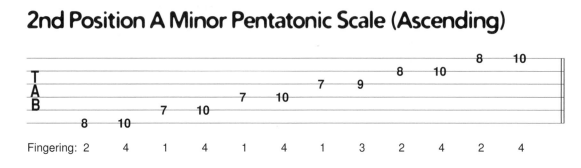

Fingering: 2   4   1   4   1   4   1   3   2   4   2   4

2nd Position A Minor Pentatonic Scale (Descending)

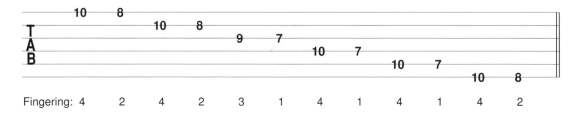

Fingering: 4   2   4   2   3   1   4   1   4   1   4   2

3rd Position A Minor Pentatonic Scale (Ascending)

3rd position

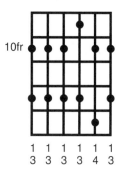

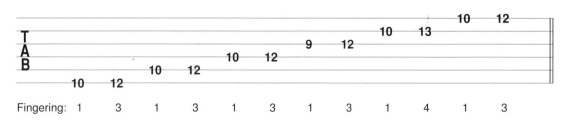

Fingering: 1   3   1   3   1   3   1   3   1   4   1   3

3rd Position A Minor Pentatonic Scale (Descending)

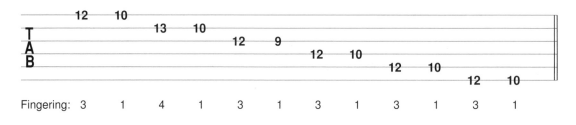

Fingering: 3   1   4   1   3   1   3   1   3   1   3   1

34

Lesson 15
Double Lead Pattern

The following example is a standard lead pattern exercise, designed to help you build coordination and learn how to begin using the minor pentatonics for playing leads. Use alternate picking and the metronome to start out slowly and get the rhythm. Memorize the pattern and gradually speed up the tempo. Before you know it, you'll be playing blazing rock and blues guitar solos.

Here is the 1st position A minor pentatonic scale played using a doubling pattern. Play the notes on the 5th through 2nd strings twice as you travel up and down the scale. Use alternate picking and a steady, even tempo.

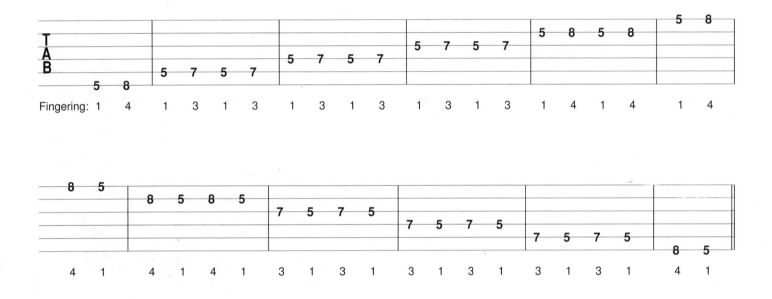

Now let's take the same double lead pattern and transpose it to the 2nd positon. Once you've got these two memorized, transpose this pattern to the 3rd position as well.

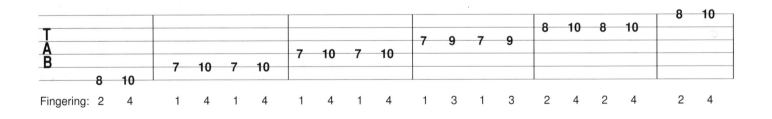

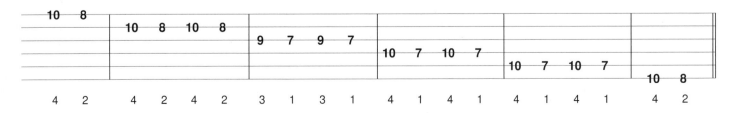

Review Quiz #2

1) The six lines of the tablature staff represent
   A. six different chords
   B. the six strings of the guitar
   C. the first six frets on the guitar
   D. nothing

2) If two or more numbers are stacked together on the tablature staff, those notes should be
   A. ignored
   B. played one at a time
   C. played backwards
   D. played together

3) 12-bar blues is
   A. a blues progression consisting of 12 measures of repeated music
   B. 12 minutes long
   C. a standard heavy metal progression
   D. always in the key of G

4) Most blues songs are played using
   A. minor chords
   B. a shuffle feel
   C. all major chords
   D. a metronome

5) Minor pentatonic scales contain
   A. five different notes
   B. only minor notes
   C. one beat
   D. seven different notes

6) Minor chords have
   A. triplets
   B. two notes
   C. a sad or melancholy sound
   D. a happy, bright sound

7) The I - IV - V chords are also called the
   A. subtonic, dominant, supertonic
   B. dominant, superdominant, subdominant
   C. tonic, dominant, superdominant
   D. tonic, sudominant, dominant

8) Chord names that contain a lowercase "m" are
   A. muted chords
   B. major chords
   C. minor chords
   D. middle chords

Answers to the review quiz are located on page 63.

Lesson 16
Introduction to Bending

Now let's learn some lead guitar techniques that will add expression to your playing. Bends are a very soulful way of creating emotion with the guitar, using flesh against steel to alter and control pitches. All guitarists have their own unique, signature way of bending notes.

The row of tab staffs below show bends using the third, fourth or first fingers. The "B" above the staff indicates a bend, and the arrow with a "1" above it means to bend the note one whole step in pitch.

First try the third finger bend. While fretting the note with your third finger, keep your first two fingers down on the string behind it and push upward using all three fingers. This will give you added coordination and control. Use the same technique for the fourth finger bend, using all four fingers to bend the string upward. The first finger bend will probably be the hardest since you are only using one finger to bend the string. In some situations, you may even pull the string downward with your first finger to bend the note.

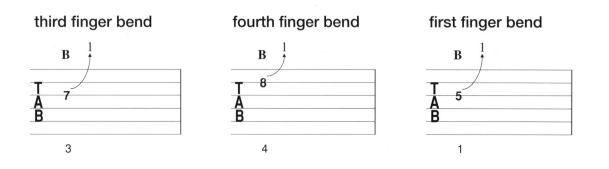

The following exercise shows what bending looks like in context when playing a solo using the 1st position A minor pentatonic scale. Play through this exercise and start to get a feel for how to incorporate bends into your own riffs.

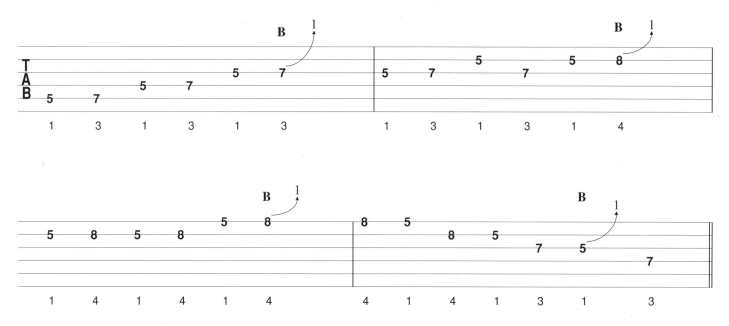

Lesson 17
Barre Chords

Two very important chords are the **F** and **B♭** barre chords. These are full barre chords containing no open strings, so they are *moveable* chords. You can transpose them to any fret.

Full barre chords are especially difficult to play. For the **F** barre chord, you need to barre your first finger across all six strings, then add the other three notes as well. Pick out each note individually to make sure it sounds clean and you've got it down. After mastering these chords, you'll be able to play in any key and position on the guitar.

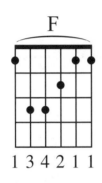

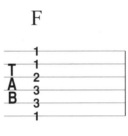

Notice that the lowest note of the chord is the root note. Using the musical alphabet and the chromatic scale chart below, you can move full barre chords up the neck and change them to any chord in the scale. Use the following chart to find any chord along the 6th string by moving the **F** chord.

6th string notes (F chord)	E	F	F♯	G	G♯	A	A♯	B	C	C♯	D	D♯	E
fret number	Open	1	2	3	4	5	6	7	8	9	10	11	12
5th string notes (B♭ chord)	A	B♭	B	C	C♯	D	D♯	E	F	F♯	G	G♯	A

For the **B♭** chord, you need to barre across three strings with your third finger. The **Fm** and **B♭m** chords are only slightly different. All of these chords are also moveable using the chart.

Fm

1 3 4 1 1 1

Fm

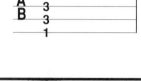

B♭

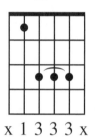

x 1 3 3 3 x

B♭

B♭m

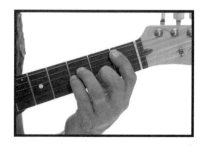

x 1 3 4 2 1

B♭m

Lesson 18
Barre Chord Rhythm #1

Rhythms for many rock songs are played using only barre chords. Learning how to comfortably change from chord to chord is essential. The following rhythm uses all barre chords and is played using a typical eighth note strumming pattern. Count along as you play to get the correct timing. Take it slow at first until you master switching from chord to chord in time and on the beat. When you've got it memorized, practice playing along with the bass and drum backing track.

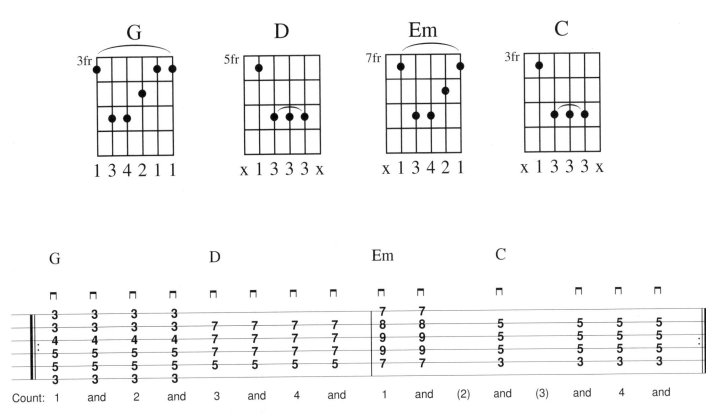

Quick Tip!

develop good practice habits

Knowing how to practice efficiently will accelerate your progress. Set aside a certain amount of time for practicing and have a routine that reviews all of the techniques you know. Create your own exercises that target weaknesses in your playing. It's important to experiment and get creative as well; try things fast or slow, light or hard, soft or loud.

Lesson 19
Barre Chord Rhythm #2

The following example is another popular rock rhythm using all barre chords. Play along to the backing track and get the quick strumming feel down. You can take all of the chords you've learned and play them in this or any other rhythm, then try writing some of your own songs.

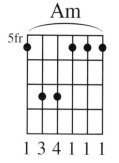
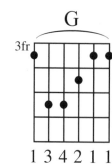
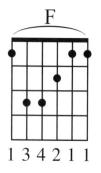

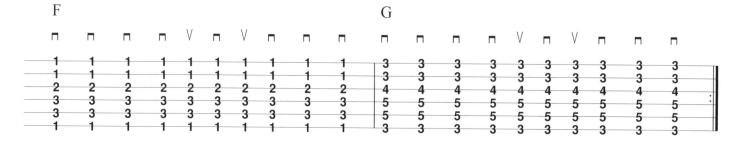

Lesson 20

Rock Riffs

Here are some familiar rock riff examples. A riff is a repeated theme, usually made up of a series of single notes. Many rock and metal songs are based on one or two simple riffs. In the following examples the left hand fingerings are shown below each tab staff. The second and third riffs have specific picking patterns that are indicated by the picking symbols above each staff.

Rock Riff #1

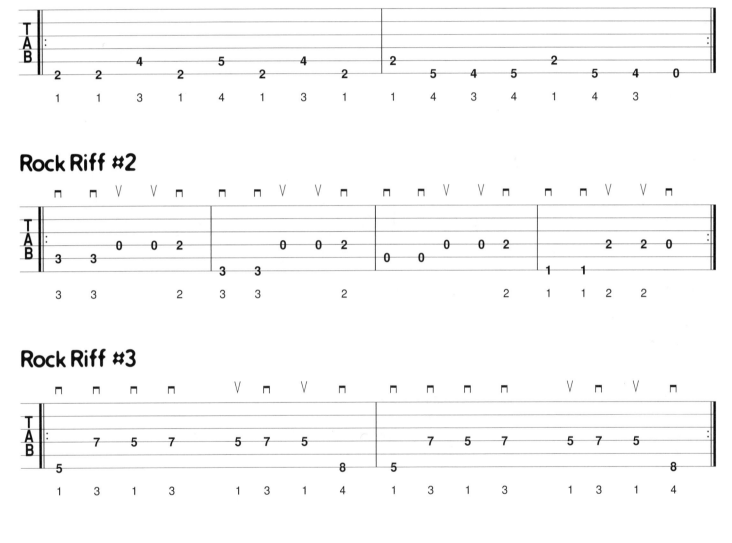

Rock Riff #2

Rock Riff #3

Rock Riff #4

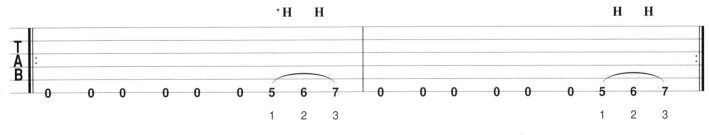

*H = Hammer on (refer to Lesson 21).

Lesson 21

Hammer On & Pull Off Exercise

Hammer ons and pull offs are two more widely used lead techniques. On the staffs below, you'll see a slur connecting one tab number to the next. This indicates that only the first tab number is picked; the second note is not struck. The "H" above the slur indicates a hammer on, and the "P" indicates a pull off.

To play a hammer on, pick the first note and then push down the next note using just your left hand finger (without picking it). Play through the series of hammer ons in the first meaure below to see how you can use these with the minor pentatonic scale.

Pull offs are the opposite of hammer ons. Pick the first note and pull or snap your finger off the string to the get the second note. Your first finger should already be in place, fretting the second note in advance.

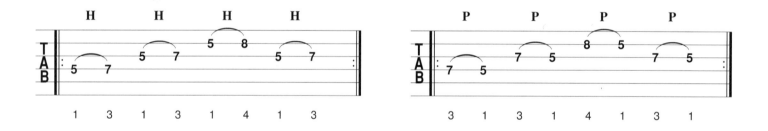

The following exercise contains hammer ons and pull offs in combination. The slurs encompass three notes, so only pick the first one. Hammer on for the second note, then pull off to the third note. At the very end of the second measure, you'll see a squiggly line above the last note. This line indicates a technique known as vibrato. While sustaining the note, shake your finger slightly and "dig in" to the note to slightly vibrate the pitch and give it more expression.

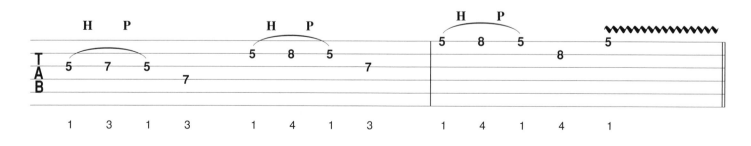

Lesson 22

Full Blues Rhythm & Lead

Full Blues Rhythm

This standard blues rhythm is in A and uses a I - IV - V progression. The rhythm is similar to Blues Rhythm #1 from Lesson 10. Be sure to keep your first finger anchored at the 2nd fret while stretching with your fourth finger to fret the notes at the 5th fret. Practice along with the backing track to get the timing and the shuffle feel.

A

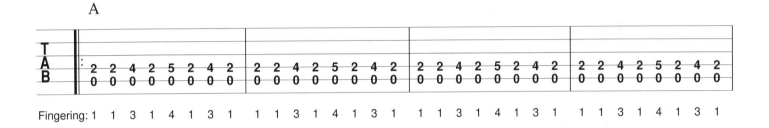

Fingering: 1 1 3 1 4 1 3 1   1 1 3 1 4 1 3 1   1 1 3 1 4 1 3 1   1 1 3 1 4 1 3 1

D   A

```
2 2 4 2 5 2 4 2    2 2 4 2 5 2 4 2
0 0 0 0 0 0 0 0    0 0 0 0 0 0 0 0                 2 2 4 2 5 2 4 2    2 2 4 2 5 2 4 2
                                                   0 0 0 0 0 0 0 0    0 0 0 0 0 0 0 0
```

1 1 3 1 4 1 3 1   1 1 3 1 4 1 3 1   1 1 3 1 4 1 3 1   1 1 3 1 4 1 3 1

E   A

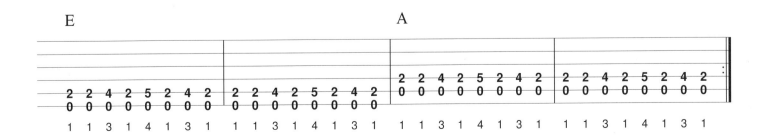

1 1 3 1 4 1 3 1   1 1 3 1 4 1 3 1   1 1 3 1 4 1 3 1   1 1 3 1 4 1 3 1

Full Blues Lead

Here's an example of a solo that can be played over the shuffle blues rhythm you've just learned. This solo incorporates bends, hammer ons and pull offs in a variety of positions. The riff in the first measure is one of the most commonly used blues riffs; it can be heard in countless blues guitar solos. The last two measures contain a *blues turnaround* (a phrase used at the end of a 12-bar blues to bring you back around to the beginning of the progression). After you've got this solo down, try to create your own using all of the lead techniques and different positions of the A minor pentatonic scales.

A

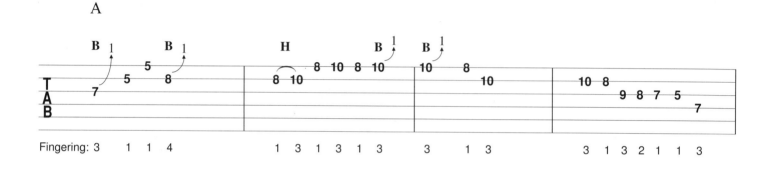

D   A

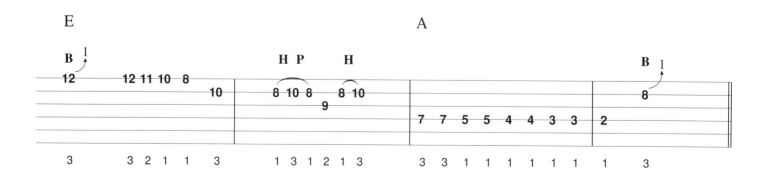

E   A

Lesson 23

Single String Picking

This exercise is designed to strengthen your picking hand and increase coordination and control of the pick. Practice this exercise using any of the open strings; you don't need your left hand for this one at all. Use consistent, steady alternate picking and play continuously for about five minutes without stopping. You can practice this anytime, even while relaxing and watching TV.

```
      ⊓ V ⊓ V ⊓ V ⊓ V ⊓ V ⊓ V ⊓ V ⊓ V    ⊓ V ⊓ V ⊓ V ⊓ V ⊓ V ⊓ V ⊓ V ⊓ V
T
A ‖: 0 0 0 0 0 0 0 0 0 0 0 0 0 0 0 0 | 0 0 0 0 0 0 0 0 0 0 0 0 0 0 0 0 :‖
B
```

Quick Tip!

play slowly at first

When learning something new, don't start out trying to play it as fast as possible. Take things slowly at first; play slow enough so you don't keep making mistakes. Build your speed over time. A great tool for learning to build speed gradually is a metronome. This is a device that clicks at an adjustable rate that you set. A metronome allows you to gauge your progress each day. By playing along with the click, you learn to play in time with other instruments.

Lesson 24

Minor Pentatonic Scales 4 – 5

Here are the last two positions of the A minor pentatonic scale. Practice and memorize both scale positions ascending and descending. You can also practice the scales using the Double Lead Pattern from Lesson 15.

4th Position A Minor Pentatonic Scale (Ascending)

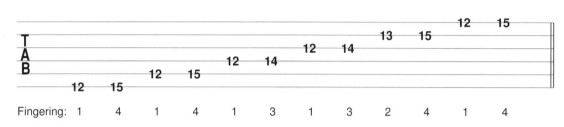

4th position

Fingering: 1   4   1   4   1   3   1   3   2   4   1   4

4th Position A minor Pentatonic Scale (Descending)

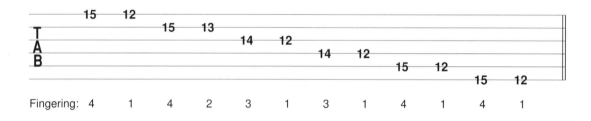

Fingering: 4   1   4   2   3   1   3   1   4   1   4   1

5th Position A minor Pentatonic Scale (Ascending)

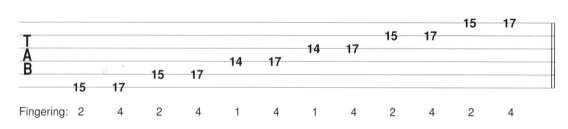

5th position

Fingering: 2   4   2   4   1   4   1   4   2   4   2   4

5th Position A Minor Pentatonic Scale (Descending)

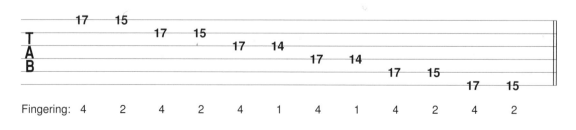

Fingering: 4   2   4   2   4   1   4   1   4   2   4   2

Minor Pentatonic Scale Fretboard Diagram

Once you have all five positions of the minor pentatonic scales mastered, you'll be able to play solos in any position on the neck. Remember that there are only five different name notes in the scale, and the different positions are just groupings of these same notes in different octaves and different places on the neck. The 4th and 5th positions from the previous page can be transposed one octave lower (shown below in the fretboard diagram). Notice how each positon overlaps the next; the left side of one position is the right side of the next one and so on. Think of these scale positions as building blocks (like Legos). When soloing, you can move from position to position and play across the entire fretboard.

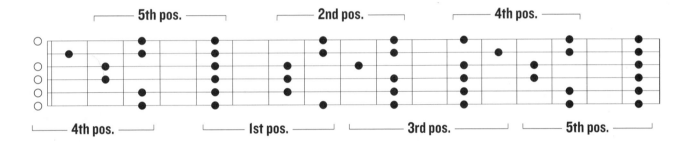

Quick Tip!

learn gradually and have realistic goals

Don't try to play a lot of things you aren't ready for. Be realistic about your capabilities as a beginner and learn gradually. If you progress at a steady, methodical rate, your technique and control of the guitar will become solid as you advance. Strive to master each new technique, chord or scale before moving on to something else. Attempting things that you're not quite ready for can discourage you instead of inspire you to play.

Lesson 25
Triplet Lead Pattern

The following triplet lead pattern exercise uses the A minor pentatonic scale played in groups of three notes, or triplets. Count "one - two - three, one - two - three" out loud while you play through this exercise to get the triplet feel in your head. Memorizing and practicing lead patterns will help you get comfortable with playing the scales in the context of leads and solos. Practice this and all lead patterns along with a metronome to develop timing and control. The first example below uses the 1st position A minor pentatonic scale ascending.

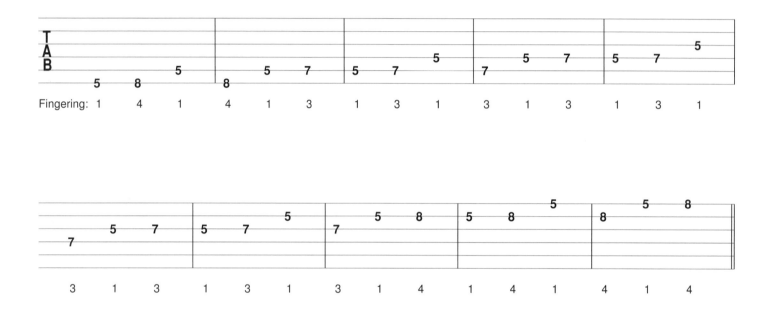

Now let's play the same pattern in reverse, back down the scale in triplets.

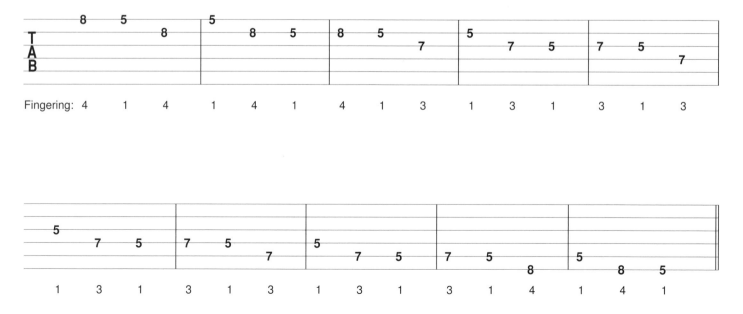

50

Practice every position of the A minor pentatonic scale using the tripet lead pattern and alternate picking. The 2nd position ascending and descending triplet patterns are shown below.

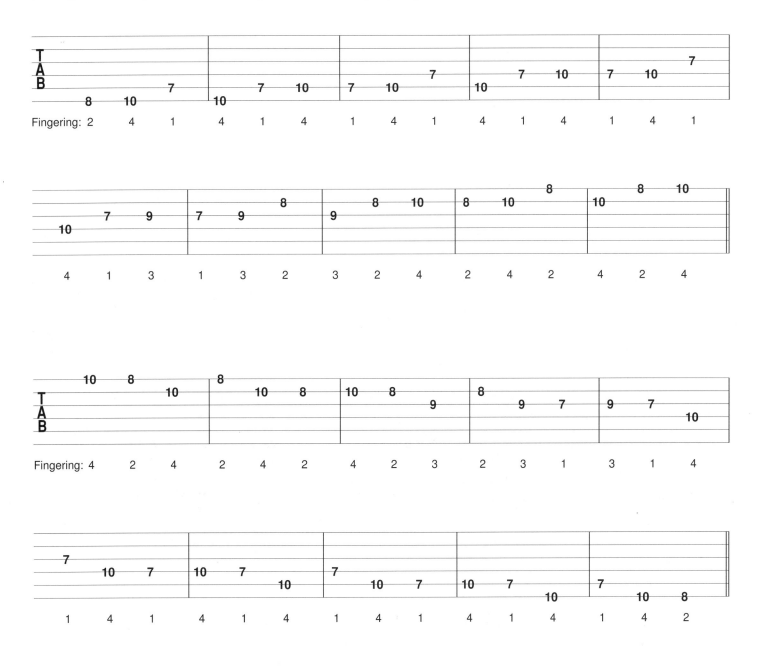

Quick Tip!

test your memory

The easiest way to memorize a piece is through repetition. The more you repeat each part, the easier it will be to hear in your head. You may find it easier to memorize something by breaking it into small sections. Be sure to have the first few bits down before moving on and memorization should begin to happen naturally.

Lesson 26

Rock Rhythm & Lead

For the last section of this program we'll use a complete rock rhythm and show you how to solo over it. First learn the rhythm part and play it along with the backing track. This is a rhythm based on barre chords in the key of A minor.

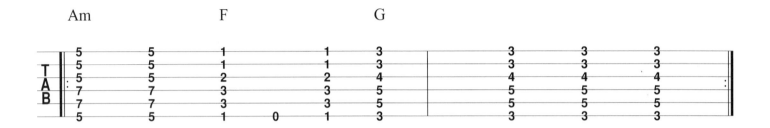

The following guitar solo incorporates all of the lead techniques and covers several positions of the minor pentatonic scale. After you've got this lead down, get creative and try improvising along with the backing track in every position of the A minor pentatonic, using bends, hammer ons and pull offs. You should now have a solid foundation for playing your own rock and blues solos.

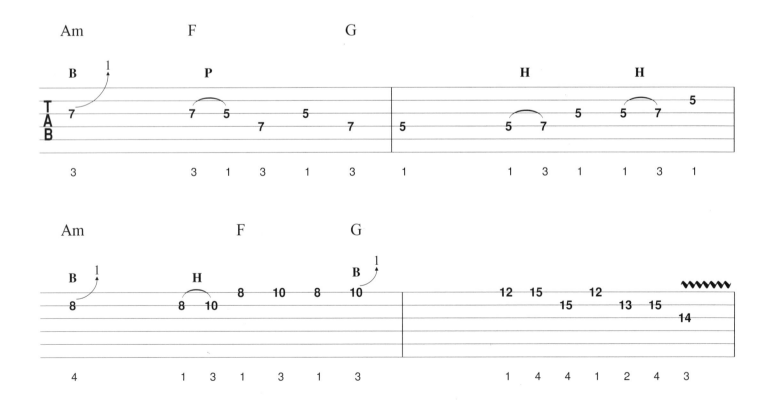

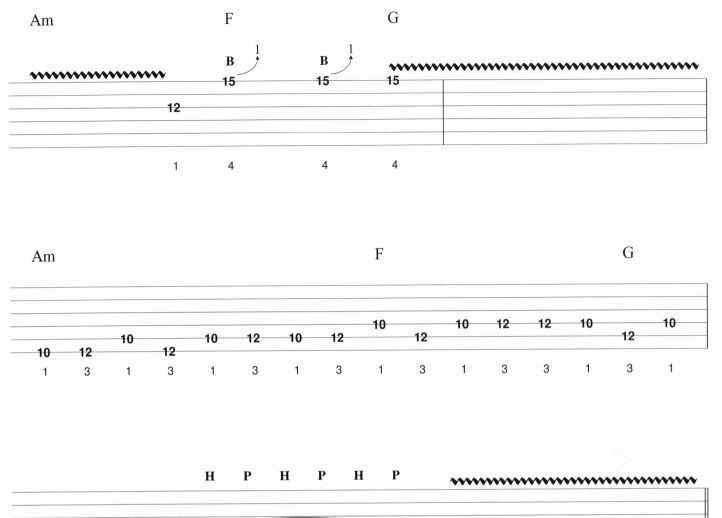

experiment and challenge your creative mind

It's great to be able to play along with your favorite recordings note for note, but you can get even more out of practicing by analyzing and experimenting with them. Isolate your favorite riffs and sections and transpose them to other keys. Try playing them at different speeds using different techniques. Hear how the notes interact with the chord progressions and apply these ideas to different situations. All of this will help you to build a well rounded improvisational vocabulary.

Review Quiz #3

1) How many different positions of the minor pentatonic scale are there?
   A. 6
   B. 3
   C. 5
   D. 7

2) Notes played in groups of three are called
   A. eighth notes
   B. whole notes
   C. syncopation
   D. triplets

3) Barre chords are
   A. moveable chords
   B. easy to play
   C. open string chords
   D. only used in jazz

4) Two frequently used lead techniques are
   A. tuning and strumming
   B. barre chords and open chords
   C. hammer ons and pull offs
   D. eighth notes and quarter notes

5) A repeated theme made up of single notes is
   A. repetitive
   B. boring
   C. a riff
   D. a pentatonic scale

6) The slight shaking of a sustained note is
   A. a hammer on
   B. vibrato
   C. a bend
   D. a shuffle

7) When playing an F barre chord, the root note is on the
   A. 2nd string
   B. 5th string
   C. 6th string
   D. 3rd string

8) The 1st position of the A minor pentatonic scale is played at the
   A. 8th fret
   B. 3rd fret
   C. 15th fret
   D. 5th fret

Answers to the review quiz are located on page 63.

Changing a String

Old guitar strings may break or lose their tone and become harder to keep in tune. You might feel comfortable at first having a teacher or someone at a music store change your strings for you, but eventually you will need to know how to do it yourself. Changing the strings on a guitar is not as difficult as it may seem and the best way to learn how to do this is by practicing. Guitar strings are fairly inexpensive and you may have to go through a few to get it right the first time you try to restring your guitar. How often you change your strings depends entirely on how much you play your guitar, but if the same strings have been on it for months, it's probably time for a new set.

Most strings attach at the headstock in the same way, however electric and acoustic guitars vary in the way in which the string is attached at the bridge. Before removing the old string from the guitar, examine the way it is attached to the guitar and try to duplicate that with the new string. Acoustic guitars may use removeable bridge pins that fasten the end of the string to the guitar by pushing it into the bridge and securing it there. On some electric guitars, the string may need to be threaded through a hole in the back of the body.

Follow the series of photos below for a basic description of how to change a string. Before trying it yourself, read through the quick tips for beginners on the following page.

Use a string winder to loosen the string.

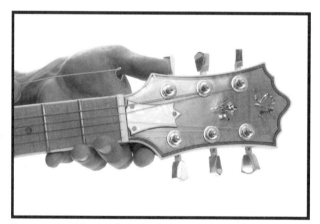
Remove the old string from the tuning post.

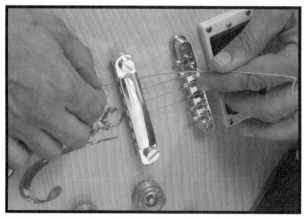
Pull the old string through the bridge and remove it from the guitar.

Remove the new string from the packaging and uncoil it.

Thread the end of the new string through the bridge.

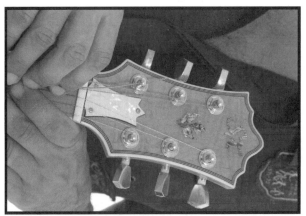

Pull the string along the neck and thread it through the small hole on the tuning post.

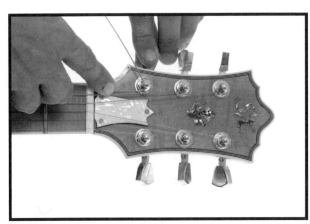

Hold the string in place just after the nut with your finger and tighten up the slack in the string with the machine head.

Carefully tighten the string and tune it to the proper pitch.

You can cut the old string off the guitar but you may want to unwind it instead and save it as a spare in case you break a string later.

Check to make sure you have the correct string in your hand before putting it on the guitar. The strings may be color coded at the end to help you identify them.

Be sure to wind the string around the tuning post in the proper direction (see photos), and leave enough slack to wind the string around the post several times. The string should wind around the post underneath itself to form a nice, neat coil.

Once the extra slack is taken up and the string is taught, tune it very gradually to pitch, being careful not to overtighten and accidentally break the new string.

Once the string is on the guitar and tightened up, you can cut the excess string sticking out from the tuning post with a wire cutter. The sharp tail end that is left can be bent downward with the wire cutter to get it out of the way and avoid cutting or stabbing your finger on it.

Check the ends of the string to make sure it is sitting correctly on the proper saddle and space on the nut.

New strings will go out of tune very quickly until they are broken in. You can gently massage the new string with your thumbs and fingers once it's on the guitar, slightly stretching the string out and helping to break it in. Then retune the string and repeat this process a few times for each string.

Guitar Solo
from Learn Rock Guitar Beginner DVD

This solo is an inspirational piece that contains many of the scales and techniques that are taught in my Learn Rock Guitar Beginner, Intermediate, and Advanced programs. When trying to learn a challenging piece you should break it down into small sections, mastering each before moving to the next. I hope you enjoy your musical journey.

- *John McCarthy*

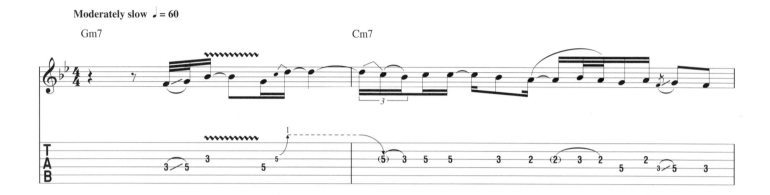

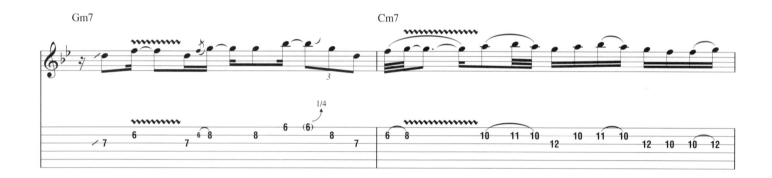

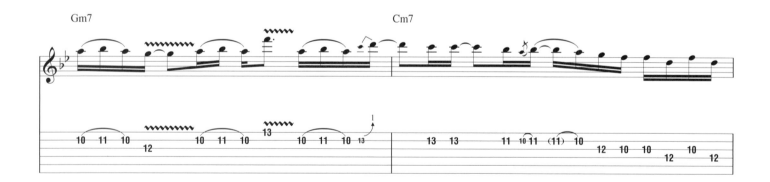

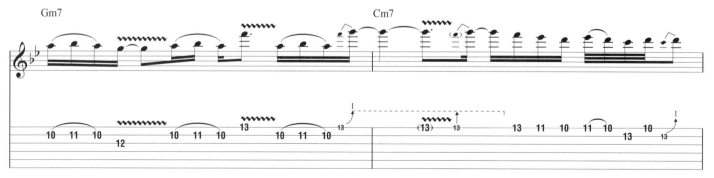

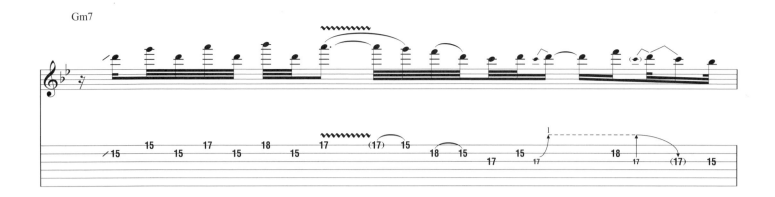

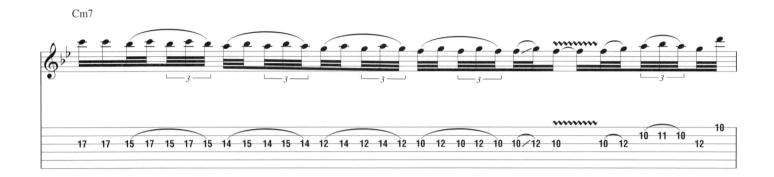

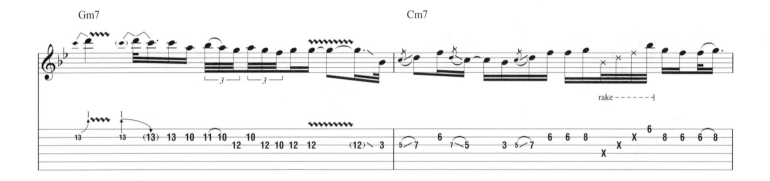

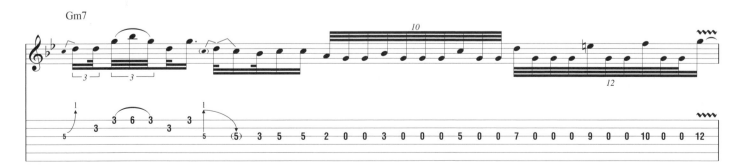

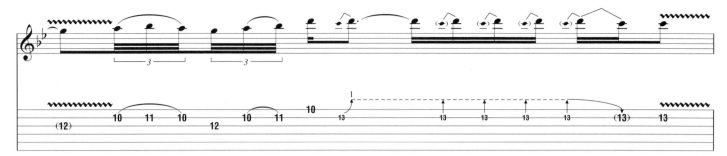

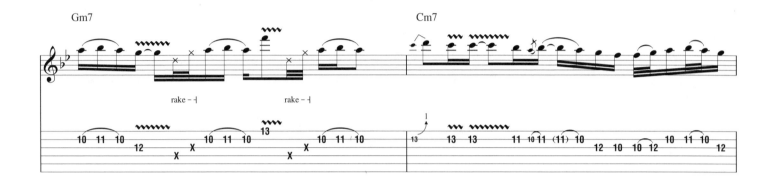

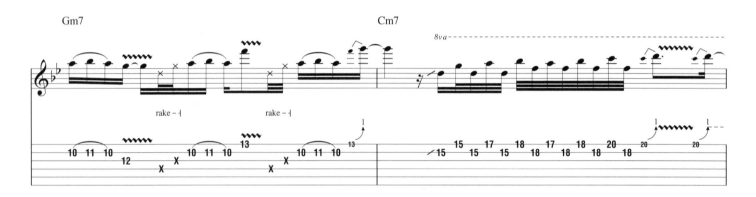

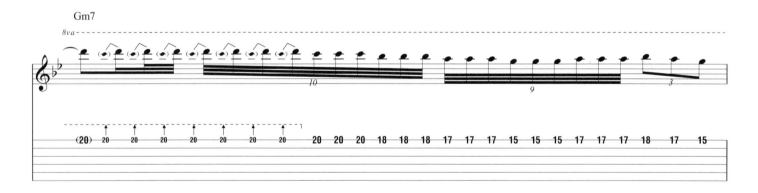

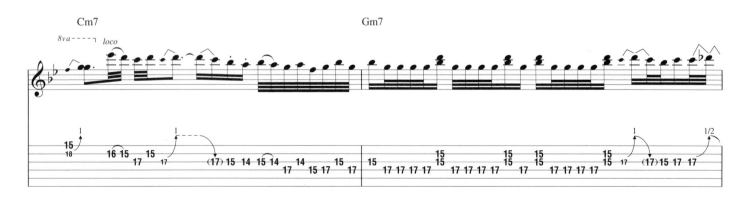

Cm7

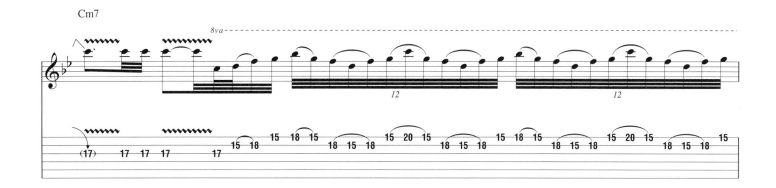

Gm7

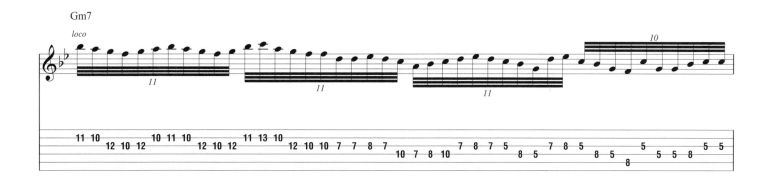

Cm7

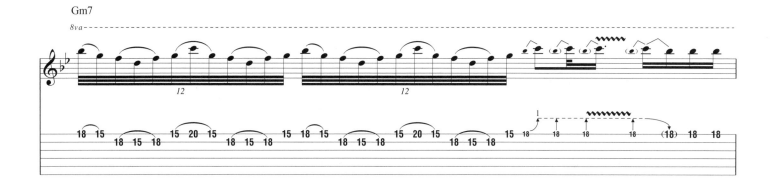

Gm7

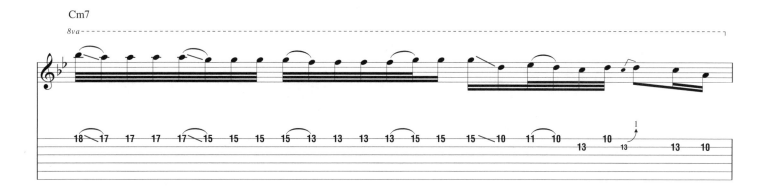

Cm7

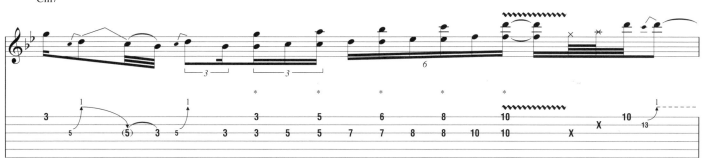

*Plucked w/ pick and fingers.

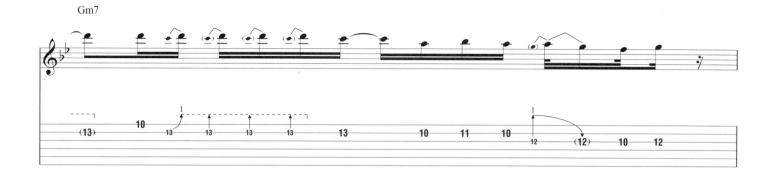

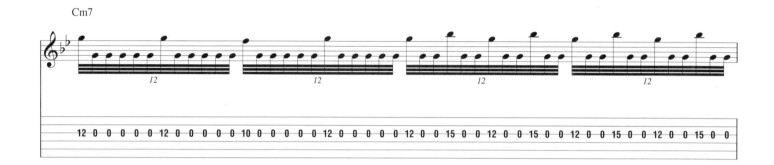

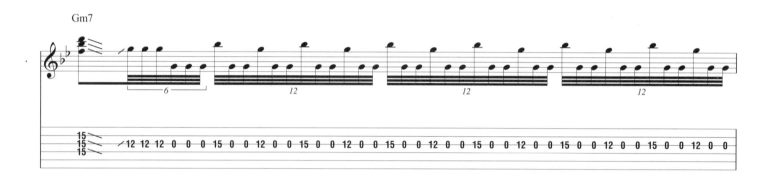

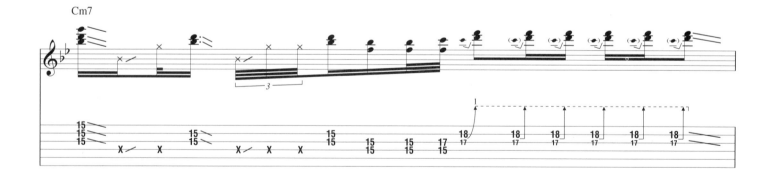

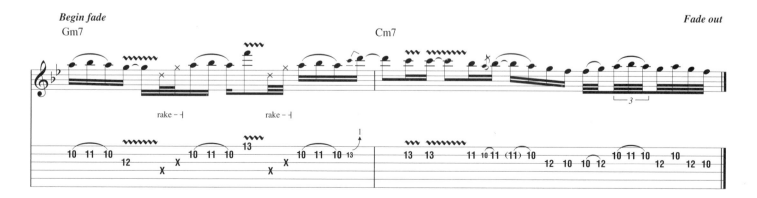

Learn Rock Guitar Beginner
CD track list & page index

Review Quiz Answer Key

Review Quiz #1

1) C

2) C

3) A

4) C

5) C

6) C

7) B

8) C

Review Quiz #2

1) B

2) D

3) A

4) B

5) A

6) C

7) D

8) C

Review Quiz #3

1) C

2) D

3) A

4) C

5) C

6) B

7) C

8) D